Basics

flattened crimp

1 Hold the crimp bead using the tip of your chainnose pliers. Squeeze the pliers firmly to flatten the crimp. Tug the clasp to make sure the crimp has a solid grip on the wire. If the wire slides, remove the crimp bead and repeat the steps with a new crimp bead.
2 Test that the flattened crimp is secure.

folded crimp

1 Position the crimp bead in the notch closest to the crimping pliers' handle.
2 Separate the wires and firmly squeeze the crimp.

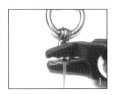 

3 Move the crimp into the notch at the pliers' tip and hold the crimp as shown. Squeeze the crimp bead, folding it in half at the indentation.
4 Test that the folded crimp is secure.

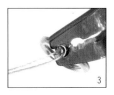 

surgeon's knot

Cross the right end over the left end and go through the loop. Go over and through again. Cross the left end over the right end and go through once. Pull the ends to tighten.

half-hitch knot

Come out of a bead and form a loop perpendicular to the thread between beads. Bring the needle under the thread away from the loop. Then go back over the thread and through the loop. Pull gently so the knot doesn't tighten prematurely.

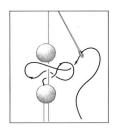

plain loops

1 Trim the wire ⅜ in. (1cm) above the top bead. Make a right-angle bend close to the bead.
2 Grab the wire's tip with roundnose pliers. Roll the wire to form a half circle. Release the wire.

3 Reposition the pliers in the loop and continue rolling.
4 The finished loop should form a centered circle above the bead.

wrapped loops

1 Make sure you have at least 1¼ in. (3.2cm) of wire above the bead. With the tip of your chainnose pliers, grasp the wire directly above the bead. Bend the wire (above the pliers) into a right angle.

2 Using roundnose pliers, position the jaws in the bend.
3 Bring the wire over the top jaw of the roundnose pliers.
4 Keep the jaws vertical and reposition the pliers' lower jaw snugly into the loop. Curve the wire downward around the bottom of the roundnose pliers. This is the first half of a wrapped loop.

5 Position the chainnose pliers' jaws across the loop.
6 Wrap the wire around the wire stem, covering the stem between the loop and the top of the bead. Trim the excess wire and press the cut end close to the wraps with chainnose pliers.

opening and closing loops and rings

1 Hold the loop or jump ring with two pairs of chainnose pliers or chainnose and roundnose pliers, as shown.
2 To open the loop or jump ring, bring one pair of pliers toward you and push the other pair away.

3 While the loop or jump ring is open, string on beads, chain, or other elements. Reverse the steps to close the opened loop or ring.

Crystal chains

Wrapped wire loops connect crystal beads securely to a cable chain in these delicate earrings. Make yours longer or shorter by adjusting the length of the chain and the corresponding number of dangles.

In a shorter length, the earrings look very tailored. Adding length makes them more dramatic. Doubling the number of dangles fills out earrings made with smaller beads. And substituting ear wires for posts presents no problem at all.

❶ String one bead onto a head pin. Make the first half of a wrapped loop (see "Basics," p. 3 and **photo a**). Since these earrings are delicate, you'll need to make a small loop that's no bigger than a link in the cable chain. Work close to the pliers' tip where the diameter of each jaw is narrowest.

❷ Slip the bottom link of the cable chain into the loop (**photo b**) and complete the wrap. Clip the wire close to the last wrap.

❸ Attach one bead to each link in the chain. When you reach the desired length, skip one link and cut the chain.

❹ Snip the head off a head pin and make a wrapped loop at one end. String a crystal onto the head pin, trim the remaining wire to ⅜ in. (1cm), and make a small plain loop (see "Basics"). Or, for additional security, make the first half of a wrapped loop instead.

❺ Attach the top link of the chain to the loop beneath the bead unit (**photo c**). If using a plain loop, close it. If using a wrapped loop, complete the wrap.

a

b

c

d

❻ Open the loop on the earring wire or post and attach it to the top loop of the crystal dangle (**photo d**). Close the loop.
❼ Make a second earring to match the first. ● – *May Frank*

Contact May in care of Kalmbach Publishing at books@kalmbach.com.

materials
- **40–50** 3–6mm crystals
- **40–50** 2-in. (5cm) head pins
- **6–8 in. (15–20cm)** 2.2mm cable chain
- **2** earring studs or wires with loop

Tools: chainnose and roundnose pliers, diagonal wire cutters

Sparkling bracelet

T urn a lively mix of crystals into a dazzling bracelet.

❶ Determine the finished length of your bracelet and cut a piece of chain to that length.

❷ String each crystal on a head pin and make the first half of a wrapped loop (see "Basics," p. 3 and **photo a**) above each.

❸ Slide a bead unit onto the chain link and complete the wraps. Continue building the bracelet, staggering sizes and colors of crystals. Work on both sides of the chain and attach several units per link for maximum fullness (**photo b**).

❹ Attach a split ring to the end link of chain. Attach half the clasp to the split ring (**photo c**). Repeat on the other end of the bracelet with the remaining clasp half. ●

– Karin Buckingham

Contact Karin in care of Kalmbach Publishing at books@kalmbach.com.

materials

- **16** or more 10mm bicone crystals
- **18** or more 8mm round crystals
- **18** or more 6mm bicone crystals
- **22** or more 6mm round crystals
- **16** or more 4mm cube crystals
- **90** or more 2-in. (5cm) head pins
- **1** ft. (30cm) dapped curb link 5.2mm chain
- **2** 6mm split rings
- toggle clasp

Tools: chainnose and roundnose pliers, diagonal wire cutters

a

b

c

Fringed heart dangles

Whether you like daring dangles or dainty drops, these earrings are the perfect pair. Start with any bead with a top-drilled hole, then make a beaded bail and embellish it with branched fringe. Create custom ear wires for a professional look.

long earrings

❶ String eight 15ºs, a crystal heart, eight 15ºs, a 4mm bicone, a 15º, a 4mm round, a 15º, a 6mm round, a 15º, a 4mm round, a 15º, a 4mm bicone, and a 15º to the middle of a 1-yd. (.9m) length of thread (**figure 1, a–b**).

❷ Pick up a jump ring and sew back through the last ten beads strung and continue through the first eight 15ºs strung in step 1 (**figure 1, b–c**).

❸ Pick up seven 15ºs, skip the last 15º, and sew back through the next two 15ºs (**figure 1, c–d**).

❹ Pick up three 15ºs, skip the last 15º, and sew back through the next two 15ºs. Then sew through the next two 15ºs of the original seven (**figure 1, d–e**).

❺ Repeat step 4 twice. Go through the next two 15ºs on the bail (**figure 1, e–f**).

❻ Repeat steps 3–5 to complete three more sets of fringe, exiting the last 15º on the bail (**figure 1, f–g**). Secure the thread with half-hitch knots between a few beads (see "Basics," p. 3).

❼ Thread a needle on the tail and sew through the eight 15ºs on the other side of the bail. Repeat the branched fringe on this side of the heart.

❽ Make a second dangle to match the first.

❾ To make your own ear wires, go to "heart ear wires" (below). Or attach the jump ring to the loop on a purchased earring finding.

short earrings

❶ String four 15ºs, a small heart, and four 15ºs. Then string an alternating pattern of three 4mm bicones and three 15ºs (**figure 2, a–b**). Slide these beads to the middle of a 1-yd. length of thread.

❷ Pick up a jump ring and sew back through the beads to **point c**.

❸ Pick up five 15ºs, skip the last 15º, and sew back through the next three 15ºs (**figure 2, c–d**).

❹ Pick up four 15ºs, skip the last 15º, and sew through the next three 15ºs. Continue through the next 15º of the original five and through the next 15º on the bail (**figure 2, d–e**).

❺ Repeat steps 3–4 to complete three more sets of fringe (**figure 2, e–f**). Secure the tail with half-hitch knots and trim.

❻ Thread a needle on the tail and sew through the four beads on the other side of the bail. Repeat steps 3–4 four times.

❼ Make a second dangle to match the first.

heart ear wires

❶ Make a right-angle bend ⅜ in. (1cm) from the end of a 4-in. (10cm) length of wire.

❷ Position your roundnose pliers at the very tip of the wire and make a curve as shown in **photo a**.

❸ Position the roundnose pliers about ¼ in. (6mm) from the bend on the long end of the wire. Bend the wire around the pliers to mirror the other side (**photo b**).

❹ Bend the long wire back on itself (**photo c**).

❺ String a 4mm bicone and form the remaining wire around a dowel to make the curve. Trim the wire to the desired length and file the end.

❻ Open the end of the heart shape, slide the soldered jump ring in, and close the heart. ● – *Anna Nehs*

Anna is an associate editor at Bead&Button. Contact her at beadbiz@hotmail.com or visit her website, beadivine.biz.

a

c

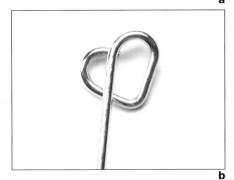

b

materials

both projects
- Silamide or Nymo D conditioned with beeswax
- beading needles, #13

long earrings
- **2** 12mm crystal hearts
- **2** 6mm round crystals
- **4** 4mm bicone crystals
- **4** 4mm round crystals
- **2g** Japanese seed beads, size 15º
- **2** 3mm soldered jump rings

short earrings
- **2** 8mm crystal hearts
- **6** 4mm bicone crystals
- **2g** Japanese seed beads, size 15º
- **2** 3mm soldered jump rings

ear wires
- **4** 4mm bicone crystals
- 16 in. (41cm) 22-gauge wire

Tools: chainnose and roundnose pliers, diagonal wire cutters, ¼ in. (6mm) dowel, metal file

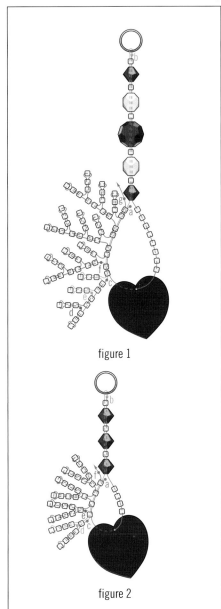

figure 1

figure 2

tip

Fringe proportions

Vary the length of the fringe to suit the size of your focal bead.

Sparkling spacers

Crystal spacers add light and definition to an easy bracelet and earring ensemble.

bracelet

1 Cut three 12-in. (31cm) strands of flexible beading wire. String a crimp bead on each strand. Crimp (see "Basics," p. 3) one strand to each loop of a clasp section (**photo a**).

2 String two 3mm silver beads, a crystal, and two cylinders on the outer (first) strand. String a silver bead, two crystals, and a cylinder on the middle (second) strand. String three crystals on the last (third) strand. Thread each strand through the corresponding hole on a spacer bar (**photo b**).

3 String three crystals on the first strand. On the second, string a cylinder, two crystals, and a cylinder. On the third, string two cylinders, a crystal, and two cylinders. Thread each strand through a spacer as before (**photo c**).

4 String two cylinders, a crystal, and two cylinders on the first strand. On the second, string a cylinder, two crystals, and a cylinder. On the third, string three crystals. Thread each strand through a spacer (**photo d**).

5 Repeat steps 3 and 4 until you've strung the last spacer bar. To finish, string two cylinders, a crystal, and two silver beads on the first strand. On the second, string a cylinder, two crystals, and a silver bead. On the third, string three crystals (**photo e**).

6 String a crimp bead on each wire. Crimp each strand to the corresponding loop on the remaining clasp section.

earrings

1 String a crystal onto a head pin. Repeat. Slide both head pins through a spacer.

2 String a crystal on one of the head pins and two crystals on the other. Go through the second spacer.

3 String a crystal on each head pin (**photo f**).

4 Trim each head pin, leaving ¼ in. (6mm) of wire above the end bead and turn a small loop (see "Basics").

5 Cut the chain in half. Count the links and remove one, if necessary, so you are working with an odd number.

6 Open one head pin loop (see "Basics") and attach the end chain link. Close the loop. Repeat with the other head pin (**photo g**).

7 Attach the ear wire to the middle chain link (**photo h**).

8 Make a second earring the mirror image of the first. ◐ – *Anna Nehs*

Anna is an associate editor at Bead&Button. *Contact her at beadbiz@hotmail.com or visit her website, beadivine.biz.*

a

b

c

d

e

f

g

h

materials

7½-in. (19cm) bracelet
- **66** 6mm crystal bicones
- **10** three-hole crystal spacers
- **6** 3mm silver beads
- **60** (approx.) Japanese cylinder beads, silver-lined
- three-strand clasp
- flexible beading wire, .014
- **6** crimp beads

Tools: crimping pliers

earrings
- **14** 6mm crystals bicones
- **4** two-hole crystal spacers
- **4** 22-gauge head pins
- **2** earring wires
- **2** in. (5cm) fine chain

Tools: roundnose and chainnose pliers, diagonal wire cutters

Tennis bracelet

Serve up the look of a classic diamond tennis bracelet with this affordable version in sparkling crystals.

❶ String a stop bead 10 in. (25cm) from the end of 2½ yd. (2.3m) of Fireline. Go through it again in the same direction.

❷ Pick up an 11º and a crystal four times. Then pick up an 11º. Go back through the first crystal and the first 11º strung (**figure 1, a–b**).

❸ Pick up a crystal, an 11º, a crystal, and an 11º. Go through the last crystal and the second-to-last 11º from the previous step (**figure 1, b–c**).

❹ Repeat step 3 as many times as

Continued on the next page

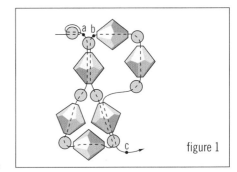

figure 1

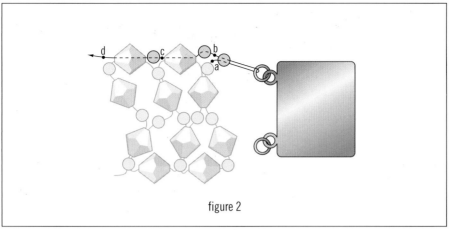

figure 2

tip

Tension

Maintaining even tension can be difficult. You may find it helps to pinch the thread next to completed steps.

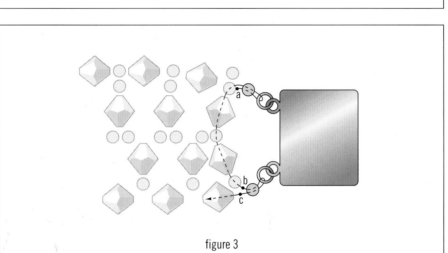

figure 3

materials

7½–in. (19cm) bracelet

- **144** 4mm Swarovski crystals
- 2g Japanese seed beads, size 11º
- two-strand box clasp
- Fireline fishing line, 6 lb. test
- beading needles, #12 or 13

necessary to make 7 in./18cm (or the desired length) of beadwork. Allow about ½ in. (1.3cm) for the clasp.

❺ Pick up an 11º, sew through one of the jump rings on the clasp, and go back through the 11º (**figure 2, a–b**).

❻ Pick up an 11º and sew through the first edge crystal (**figure 2, b–c**). Pick up an 11º and sew through the next edge crystal (**figure 2, c–d**). Continue adding 11ºs between each edge crystal until you reach the other end of the bracelet, exiting the last edge crystal.

❼ Repeat step 5 to add the other half of the clasp to this end of the bracelet. Weave through the end 11ºs and the crystals, and exit the 11º after the last crystal (**figure 3, a–b**). Remove the stop bead.

❽ Pick up an 11º, sew through the other jump ring on the clasp, and back through the 11º (**figure 3, b–c**).

❾ Sew through the first edge crystal, and then add an 11º between each edge crystal.

❿ Repeat step 8 at the other end.

⓫ Sew through all the beads along the edge and the jump rings on the clasp again to reinforce them.

⓬ Secure the tail with half-hitch knots (see "Basics," p. 3) between a few beads and trim the tail. Secure the other tail in the same manner. ◗

– Diane Hertzler

Contact Diane at P.O. Box 611, Mt. Gretna, Pennsylvania 17064, (717) 964-3071, or email her at dianehertzler@dejazzd.com.

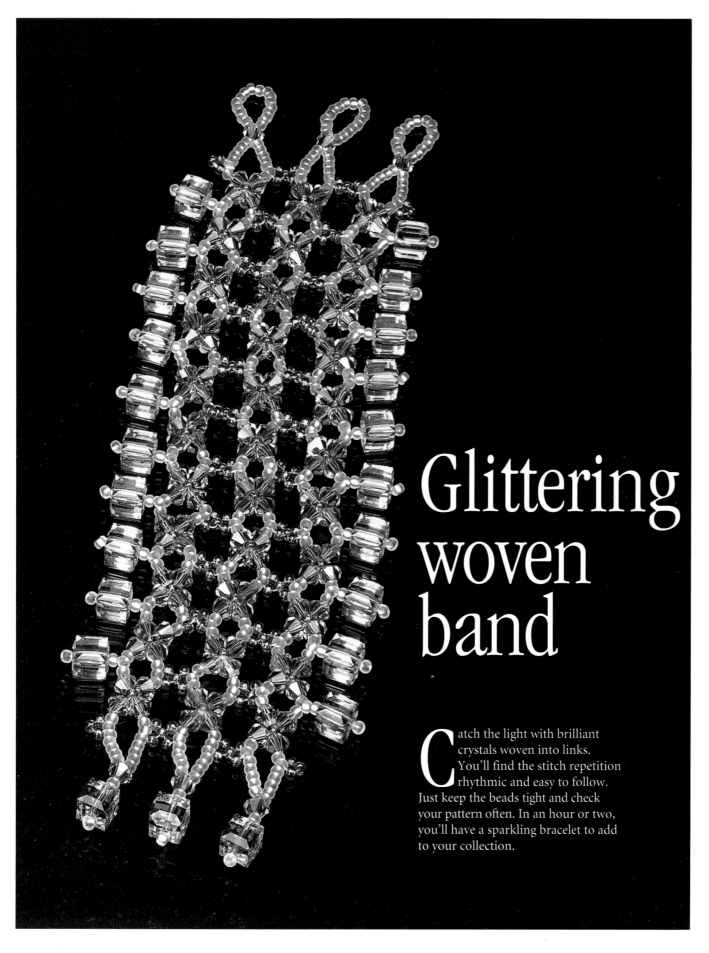

Glittering woven band

Catch the light with brilliant crystals woven into links. You'll find the stitch repetition rhythmic and easy to follow. Just keep the beads tight and check your pattern often. In an hour or two, you'll have a sparkling bracelet to add to your collection.

a

b

c

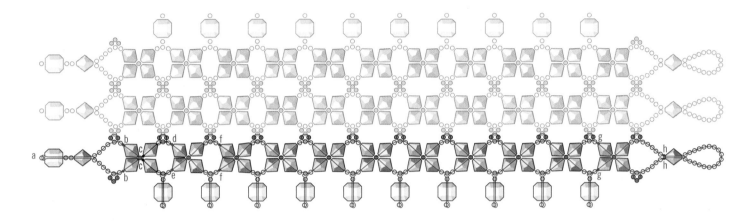

crystal button

❶ Cut 2½ yd. (2.3m) of Power Pro. Thread a needle on each end.

❷ Center a color A size 11º seed bead on the thread. String a 6mm crystal cube, two color A 11ºs, and a main color (MC) crystal over both needles.

❸ String six color A 11ºs and three color B 11ºs on one needle. Go back through the last color A 11º and tighten, forming a picot with the color B beads. String one more color A 11º. Repeat with the other needle (**photo a**).

center strand

❶ String an MC crystal and a color B 11º on one needle. On the other needle, string an MC crystal, then go through the color B 11º (**photo b**). Pull the thread to tighten the beads.

❷ String an MC crystal, two color A 11ºs, and three color B 11ºs on one needle. Go through the last color A 11º, forming a picot. Add another color A 11º. Repeat with the other needle (**photo c**).

❸ Repeat steps 1–2, using accent color (AC) crystals instead of MCs (**photo d**).

❹ Repeat steps 1–3 four times.

❺ Repeat steps 1–2, then string four color A 11ºs on each needle.

loop closure

Make a loop that fits snugly over your 6mm crystal cube bead. If you select something other than a 6mm cube, alter your loop's seed bead count.

❶ String an MC crystal and 18 color A 11ºs on both needles. Go back though the crystal in the opposite direction (**photo e**).

❷ Make a surgeon's knot (see "Basics," p. 3). Go back through the loop's 11ºs and crystal, then make another knot.

❸ Dot the knots with glue, sew through several more beads, and trim.

edge strands

Refer to the illustration above for this section. To keep the beads flat and snug, pin the bracelet to your work surface.

❶ Repeat the "crystal button" steps, but alter one picot to connect it to the center strand. To do this, pick up one color B 11º, go through the center B on the finished strand's first picot, and pick up one more color B 11º. Sew through the last color A 11º and string one more color A 11º (**a–b**).

❷ Repeat step 1 of the center strand, using AC crystals (**b–c**).

❸ On the needle next to the center strand, string an AC crystal, two color A 11ºs, and one color B 11º. Connect it to the center strand, then continue as before (**c–d**).

❹ On the other thread, string an AC crystal, three color A 11ºs, a 6mm crystal cube, and a color A 11º. Go back through the crystal cube and an 11º. Cross through the next 11º, then string one more 11º (**c–e**).

❺ Repeat steps 2–4, using MC crystals (**d–f, e–f**).

❻ Repeat steps 2–5 four times (**f–g**).

❼ Repeat step 5 of the center strand, connecting the last picot (**g–h**).

❽ Repeat the loop closure steps.

❾ Repeat steps 1–8 to make the other edge the mirror image of the first. ❍
– *Ellen Sadler*

To alter the length of this 7-in. (18cm) cuff, add or subtract design repeats.

d

e

tip

Conditioning thread

Conditioning straightens and strengthens your thread and also helps it resist fraying, separating, and tangling. Pull unwaxed nylon threads, such as Nymo, through either beeswax (not candle wax or paraffin) or Thread Heaven to condition. Beeswax adds tackiness that is useful if you want your beadwork to fit tightly. Thread Heaven adds a static charge that causes the thread to repel itself, so it shouldn't be used with doubled thread. All nylon threads stretch, so maintain tension on the thread as you condition it.

materials

7-in. (18cm) bracelet

- 2g size 11º Japanese seed beads, each of two colors
- **72** 4mm bicone crystals, main color (MC)
- **68** 4mm bicone crystals, accent color (AC)
- Power Pro beading thread, 30 lb. test
- **23** 6mm faceted crystal cubes
- beading needles, #10 or 12

Contact Ellen by mail at 123 West 93rd St. #2B, New York, NY 10025 or by email at ellensadler@juno.com.

Razzle dazzle choker

Deep down inside, many of us harbor a secret desire to dress up like a beautiful fairy princess. This choker was inspired by the secret fantasy that so many of us have treasured.

getting started

Bead a row of figure 8s to the desired length, then complete the additional rows. You can make a narrower version by not adding rows. Insert the memory wire, adding seed beads to fill in the gaps, then add two "V" drops at center front.

making the net

Thread a needle with 2 yd. (1.8m) of Nymo. Fireline is not flexible enough to accommodate the memory wire.

1 String seven seeds, a 6mm crystal, and three seeds.

2 Go through the fourth seed to make the top half of the figure 8 (**photo a** and **figure 1, a–b**).

3 String three seeds and another 6mm crystal (**figure 1, b–c**).

4 Go through seven seeds as shown in **figure 1, c–d** to create the bottom half of the figure 8.

5 String one 6mm crystal (**figure 1,** d–e). Go through seven seeds (**figure 2, a–b**). Sew straight down through the crystal again, exiting at the bottom (**figure 2, b–c**).

6 String seven seeds and go back through the crystal again from top to bottom (**figure 2, c–d**).

7 Go back up through the seven seeds again (**figure 2, d–e** and **photo b**).

8 String one 6mm crystal and three seeds. Go down the fourth seed on the seven-seed loop from step 6 (**figure 2, e–f**).

9 Repeat steps 3–8 to create the first row of interlocking figure 8s, ending with step 4. Thirty-two figure 8s will make a choker that's about 15 in. (38cm) long. When you reach the end, it is very important to reinforce the final figure 8 by sewing through it again for stability.

adding rows

Start the next row using the top crystals of the first row as the bottom crystals of the new row.

❶ At the end of row 1, the needle exits **point a** in **figure 3**. String seven seeds and loop back through the top crystal (**figure 3, a–b**).

❷ Go up through the first four seeds (**figure 3, b–c**). String three seeds, one crystal, and three seeds (**figure 3, c–d**).

❸ Go back through the fourth seed and through three more seeds (**figure 3, d–e**). You are now ready to continue the pattern beginning with step 5 from "making the net." This time, after stringing the vertical crystal, go down through the seven seeds between **points f–g on figure 3**. Then sew back up through the vertical crystal (**figure 3, g–h**). Once you've made the first figure 8 of the second row, you can turn the work so you are still beading from left to right if that's more comfortable.

❹ Add a third row of figure 8s to row 2.

starting a new thread

Tie all knots near the vertical crystals to make it easier to insert the memory wire. Knots next to horizontal crystals could block them.

When you are about to run out of thread, drop your old thread, leaving the needle on the thread. Thread a new needle, tying your old thread to your new one with a surgeon's knot (see "Basics," p. 3) as close to the beadwork as possible. After you have added several repeats, pick up your old needle and take it through the same beads. Tie another surgeon's knot as close to your work as possible. Sew through a few beads with the old thread and remove the needle. Continue on with your new thread. Leave your tails hanging. Don't glue the knots until you're sure you'll have no need to go through those beads again.

a   b

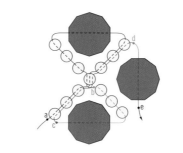

figure 1

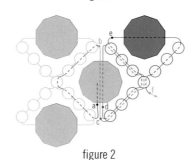

figure 2

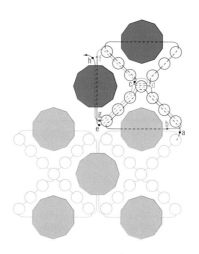

figure 3

stringing memory wire

Memory wire will ruin your tools if you try to cut it. Bend it back and forth with chainnose pliers until it snaps off. Make a loop at one end of each of the four wires with roundnose pliers and work them through the horizontal crystals, adding four or five seeds between each crystal to fill in the gaps. Make a loop at

materials

- approximately **230** 6mm round faceted crystals
- **10** 4mm round faceted crystals
- **2** 8mm crystal bicones
- 10g size 11° Japanese seed beads
- Nymo D beading thread
- beeswax
- beading needles, #12
- memory wire, **4** choker-length pieces
- G-S Hypo Cement

Tools: chainnose and roundnose pliers

the end of each wire after going through the last horizontal crystal.

the "V" drops

❶ Find the center point of your choker. The smaller, inner V will extend from the outer edge of the two crystals on either side of the center.

❷ Thread your needle with a few feet of thread and weave it through nearby beads, tying several half-hitch knots (see "Basics"). Knot it around the memory wire where it exits the first crystal.

❸ String one seed, one 4mm crystal, one seed, one 6mm crystal, one seed, one 8mm crystal, and three seeds. Sew back up through the 8mm crystal.

❹ String one seed, one 6mm crystal, one seed, one 4mm crystal, and one seed.

❺ Wrap your thread around the memory wire at the point where the V rejoins the choker and weave the thread back through the nearby beads, knotting between beads.

❻ Repeat step 1 above, starting the larger V at the inside edge of the crystals just past the one where your began the small V.

❼ Alternately string one seed and one 4mm crystal four times, then one seed, one 6mm crystal, one seed, one 8mm crystal, and three seeds. Sew back up through the 8mm crystal and string the second half of the V to mirror the first.

❽ Repeat step 5.

❾ Once the choker is completed, put a dot of glue on all your knots and trim the tails. ❍ – *Melody MacDuffee*

Melody is a frequent contributor to Bead&Button. Contact her by email at writersink@msn.com.

Royal woven neckpiece

Richly colored crystals nestled in sparkling seed beads come together to make a necklace befitting a queen.

centerpiece

Start a new length of thread for each row.

❶ Thread a needle on both ends of a 1-yd. (.9m) length of conditioned Nymo (see tip on p. 13). Pick up four seed beads and a 6mm crystal with the first needle and slide the beads to the center of the thread. Using the second needle, pick up three seeds and sew through the fourth (**figure 1**).

❷ Pick up three seeds and one 6mm crystal on each needle. Sew through seven seeds with the first needle. Repeat with the second needle (**figure 2**).

❸ Pick up a 6mm crystal and cross the needles through it in opposite directions (**figure 3**). This completes one unit.

❹ Pick up three seeds with each needle, then cross the needles through a fourth seed bead.

❺ Complete five units.

❻ Secure the tails with half-hitch knots (see "Basics," p. 3) between the beads and trim the excess thread.

❼ Work row 2 the same as row 1 with the following change in step 2: Pick up a new 6mm crystal on the first needle and go through the 6mm crystal from row 1 with the second needle (**figure 4**). Continue row 2 until there are five complete units.

❽ Refer to **figure 5** as you work the following rows:

Row 3: Complete three units.

Row 4: Center a new thread on the second edge crystal on row 1 and work two units.

Row 5: Work two units.

❾ Exit an edge 6mm crystal on the centerpiece. Pick up a 5mm crystal and go through the next edge 6mm crystal.

Continue adding crystals around the edge (**figure 5**).

neckstrap

❶ Center a 2-yd. (1.8m) length of conditioned thread on the middle 5mm crystal on row 5 (**figure 5, a–b**).

❷ Work the strap using 4mm crystals and seed beads until it is 20 units long. On the last unit, don't add the third crystal.

❸ Sew through the jump rings on the clasp. Retrace the thread path for the last unit to secure the clasp (**photo at right**).

❹ Exit the first edge 4mm crystal next to the clasp. Pick up a 3mm crystal and a seed bead. Sew through the next edge 4mm crystal. Continue adding a 3mm and a seed bead between each 4mm along the inside and outside edge of the neck strap.

❺ Repeat steps 1–4 on the other side of the centerpiece.

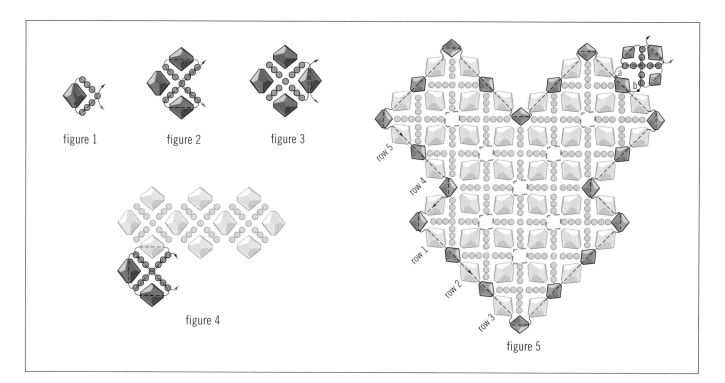

figure 1

figure 2

figure 3

figure 4

figure 5

earrings

❶ Start the same as the centerpiece, steps 1–5, using 4mm crystals and seed beads.

❷ Use one tail to attach a soldered jump ring. Exit the edge 4mm crystal on one end, pick up three beads and the jump ring, and sew back through the third bead.

❸ Pick up two beads and sew through the opposite 4mm crystal.

❹ Repeat step 4 from the neck strap along the edge of the earring using the other tail.

❺ Open the loop on an earring finding (see "Basics") and attach the jump ring to it. Close the loop.

❻ Repeat steps 1–5 to make the second earring to match the first. ◐
– Melody MacDuffee

Melody is a frequent contributor to Bead&Button. Reach her by email at writersink@msn.com.

materials

both projects
• Nymo D conditioned with beeswax
• beading needles, #12

15-in. (38cm) necklace
• Swarovski bicone crystals
  44 6mm
  28 5mm
  118 4mm
  76 3mm
• 5g Japanese seed beads, size 11º
• two-strand box clasp

earrings
• Swarovski bicone crystals
  36 4mm
  20 3mm
• 1g Japanese seed beads, size 11º
• **2** 3mm soldered jump rings
• **2** post earring findings
Tools: chainnose pliers

tip

Shaping the neckstrap

Pull the inside thread slightly tighter than the outside thread when adding 3mm crystals to create a gentle curve.

Multistrand collar

String crystals and seed beads together for a sparkling collar with a dramatic dangle.

❶ String a 3mm crystal, the focal bead, and a 4mm crystal on a head pin. Make a wrapped loop (see "Basics," p. 3) above the top bead (**photo a**).

❷ To make the pendant, cut two 7-in. (18cm) strands of .010 beading wire. String a 2-in. (5cm) alternating pattern of 3mm crystals on each strand, reversing the colors on the second strand. String a crimp bead over both wires, then string 1 in. (2.5cm) of cylinder beads on each strand (**photo b**).

❸ String the bottom right wire through the loop on the dangle and go through all the crystals on the left. Continue through the crimp bead and through a few cylinder beads. Repeat with the bottom left wire, working in the opposite direction. String the top wires through the crimp bead and through a few